CONTENTS

Some words are shown in bold, **like this**. You can find out what they mean by looking in the glossary.

Don't forget

These boxes will give you handy tips and remind you what to take on your rainforest adventures.

Amazing facts

Check out these boxes for amazing rainforest facts and figures.

Who's who

Find out more about rainforest experts and explorers of the past.

Conservation

Learn about conservation issues relating to rainforests.

INTO THE JUNGLE

You find yourself in the middle of one of the biggest forests on Earth. Giant trees reach up to the sky, which is almost invisible above the dense green forest. All around you are the buzzes and shrieks of a huge variety of animals. The hot, **humid** air is almost overpowering.

You are in a **tropical** rainforest. These forests are home to a greater variety of plants and animals than any other environment on the planet. The forests are so thick that many areas may never have been visited by another human, and certainly many of the **species** of animals and plants in the forest have not yet been recorded by scientists.

The deadly anaconda measures up to 12 metres (40 feet) in length. They wrap their coils around large **mammals** to **suffocate** them.

Amazing facts

Tropical rainforests cover about 7 per cent of Earth's land area. In 1800, rainforests covered twice the area that they cover today.

An explorer's dream

Tropical rainforests are incredibly exciting to explore. You never know what you might find next. You also need to look out – the animals and plants of the rainforest can be dangerous for a careless explorer.

Don't forget

Travel light in the hot, humid rainforest. Make sure you take:

- Clothes made of fast-drying materials that will keep you cool and protect you from the rain that falls every day.
- Medicines and protection from snake and insect bites, including a mosquito net to protect you while you sleep. A mosquito bite can pass on the deadly disease **malaria**.

What can you see along a riverbank? Find out on pages 10–11.

Find out why frogs such as this one are under threat on page 23.

Learn more about rainforest destruction on pages 34–35.

WHERE TO START

To find the world's greatest rainforests, you need to travel to the tropics. These are the regions close to the equator. Tropical rainforests are the place to find the biggest variety of life. You may not know that there are also temperate rainforests that receive lots of rain, such as the northwest Pacific coasts of the United States and parts of Australia. These are rainforests, but they are not tropical.

Mountain gorillas live in Africa's **cloud forests**. These mountain rainforests are always covered by clouds and fog.

The world's biggest rainforest is around the River Amazon in South America. Central Africa is also home to vast areas of rainforest. In Asia, lush rainforests spread across the countries of Southeast Asia, such as Indonesia and Thailand, and even into northern Australia.

 Conservation

Earth's climate is getting warmer because of gases such as **carbon dioxide** released into the **atmosphere** by human industry. Rainforest plants absorb carbon dioxide from the atmosphere, release **oxygen** that we need to breathe, and slow down the process of **climate change**.

When to go

The weather in rainforests is similar all year round. Temperatures are always high near the equator, and rainforests feel even hotter because the air is very humid. Rain falls every day in rainforests, often in violent thunderstorms.

Amazing facts

Every year, around 200 centimetres (80 inches) of rain falls in the Amazon rainforest. That's about 5 millimetres (0.2 inches) every day, which is nearly three times the amount of rain that falls in London.

Be prepared for lots of rain in rainforests like this one in Australia.

Rainforest rivers

At the heart of many rainforests are some of the world's greatest rivers. The biggest of all is the River Amazon in South America. The River Congo runs through Africa's rainforests. These mighty rivers are the highways of the forest and the best way to travel if you don't want to be fighting your way through the trees and plants.

Amazing facts

The River Amazon pours 770 billion litres (170 billion gallons) of water into the Atlantic Ocean every hour. It is 240 kilometres (150 miles) wide when it reaches the Atlantic Ocean and 16 kilometres (10 miles) wide at Manaus, when it is still 1,600 kilometres (1,000 miles) from the sea.

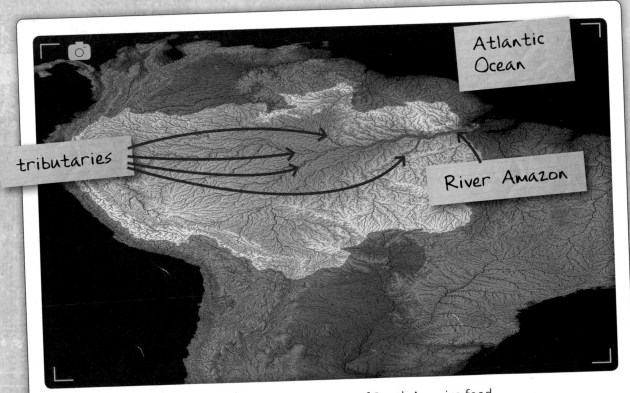

Atlantic Ocean

tributaries

River Amazon

Many tributaries that snake through the rainforests of South America feed the Amazon.

Rainforest rivers are fed by the daily rain. The large amount of water causes rivers such as the Amazon and the Congo to flow quickly. To travel along these rivers, you'll need a strong, stable boat. After all, you don't want to **capsize** and find yourself in the dangerous waters. Your boat should have some shelter from the pouring rain and burning Sun of the tropics.

Don't forget

Don't try swimming in rainforest rivers. You may find some very nasty surprises:

- Black caiman: These giant relatives of the alligator are about 4.5 metres (15 feet) long, incredibly strong, and armed with razor-sharp teeth. They can eat large mammals, including tasty explorers!
- Piranhas: These fearsome fish hunt in packs. They can strip meat off their **prey** in minutes.
- Electric eel: These unusual river animals will give you a shock – literally. They kill their prey by giving them an electric shock.

EXPLORERTRAVEL GUIDES

Along the banks

Travelling down a rainforest river will give you a great view of what's happening along the riverbank. You may catch sight of a crocodile or caiman looking out for its lunch, lying as still as possible so they look just like a fallen tree on the bank.

South American capybaras are like huge guinea pigs, weighing around 66 kilograms (145 pounds). If you startle one, they may dive into the water, where they can stay submerged for five minutes.

 ## Conservation

Rainforests contain as many as two-thirds of all animal and plant species found on Earth. This **biodiversity** means that rainforests are vitally important **ecosystems**.

Rainforest mammals will emerge from the forest to drink from the river. Tapirs are shaped like pigs, but are related to horses and rhinos. They are very shy and will usually only come out at dawn and dusk. In Asian rainforests, you may see a tiger by the river. Don't assume you're safe on your boat. Tigers can swim, and the rare Sumatran tiger even has webbed feet to help it swim faster.

Nightfall

Rainforests are usually quite dark under the dense **canopy** of trees. It could take you a while to get used to sleeping in the jungle, as the noise from forest animals does not stop just because it's night-time.

Who's who

On 9 August 2010, Ed Stafford (born 1973) reached the Atlantic Ocean. It was the end of a remarkable journey in which Stafford had walked the length of the River Amazon. He actually walked further – 9,656 kilometres (6,000 miles) – because of flooding. He was accompanied most of the way by Peruvian forest worker Gadiel "Cho" Sanchez Rivera. During the 860-day journey, they met hostile people and poisonous snakes, and ate piranha and smoked tortoise.

DISCOVERING THE RAINFORESTS

Rainforests provided many of the things early peoples needed to survive, such as food and shelter. As a result, **civilizations** grew in the forests around the world.

The population of the Amazon in 1500 was probably about 6 million people, which is many more than live there now. Many of these people were killed by diseases or conflict when Europeans arrived to explore the rainforest.

The first European explorers of the Amazon were searching for gold, spices, and other precious goods. They had little interest in the animals and plants of the region, or the culture of the people who lived there.

Amazing facts

Early explorers told stories about what they found. Francisco de Orellana (see opposite) told of a tribe of warrior women, which he called the Amazons, giving the river its name. Others searched for great riches and a place they called El Dorado (the golden one). El Dorado was thought to be somewhere near the mouth of the Orinoco River in what is now Venezuela.

Who's who

Francisco de Orellana (1490–1546) was the first European to travel the length of the River Amazon. He was one of the earliest Spanish **conquistadors** who invaded Peru and set out on an expedition to explore further east in 1541. Orellana ordered his men to build a boat and drifted along the river to the Atlantic Ocean. Orellana died when his ship sank on a second trip to the Amazon.

In the footsteps of Spanish explorers such as Francisco de Orellana, came other Europeans seeking their fortune. England's Walter Raleigh led an expedition into the forest up the Orinoco River. Raleigh was trying to win Queen Elizabeth I's favour, so he set out to try to find El Dorado. Unfortunately, his expedition was not a success. The expedition was attacked by native peoples and also alligators!

Into Africa

The search for gold in the South American rainforest continued for hundreds of years. Africa's jungles were not fully explored by non-Africans until the 1800s. Some of these explorers were driven by the search for wealth or empire-building for their home countries. Missionaries such as David Livingstone wanted to bring Christianity to Africa.

Livingstone explored much of East Africa. As a doctor, he took note of the many natural medicines that local people used from the rainforests. He was also one of the first people to warn about the destruction of rainforests.

Who's who

Henry Morton Stanley (1841–1904) moved from Wales to the United States when he was 18. After many adventures, he became a journalist for the *New York Herald*. In 1869, he was sent to "find Livingstone". He met the famous explorer in 1871. Stanley began his own explorations of Africa in 1874, including going on a journey down the River Congo. Even by the standards of his time, Stanley had a brutal approach to the Africans who helped in his expeditions.

The River Congo flows for 4,700 kilometres (2,900 miles) through the world's second-largest rainforest in central Africa.

Finding new medicines

In South America, other explorers had also realized that the riches of the rainforest were about more than just gold. The bark of the cinchona tree was recognized as a treatment for malaria. Eventually, seeds from the Amazon rainforest were planted around the world to ensure supplies of this medicine.

Amazing facts

Millions of rainforest people were killed by diseases they caught from Europeans, such as measles and smallpox. European explorers also suffered from diseases such as malaria and yellow fever, caught from mosquito bites.

Modern exploration

In modern times, exploration of the rainforests has focused on the extraordinary natural wealth of these regions. Although the rainforests have largely been mapped, there are still many areas that have not been fully explored by scientists.

American **botanist** Richard Schultes explored the Amazon in the mid-1900s. He brought back thousands of unknown plant **specimens** and documented how the region's people used plants as medicines. A modern explorer, Lou Jost, works in the cloud forests of Ecuador, recording species of **orchid** that only grow in a single valley.

Exploring the rainforest is not always glamorous. This scientist is collecting gorilla poo.

Modern explorers are often driven by the idea that they have to explore the world's rainforests and record undiscovered species of plants and animals before it is too late. Rainforests are threatened by human industry and farming, as well as by changes in climate.

Who's who

Today, explorers look for new and challenging ways to experience the rainforests. Martin Strel (born 1954) took this to extremes in 2007, when he swam 5,268 kilometres (3,274 miles) from the source of the Amazon to the ocean. Swimming an average of 80 kilometres (nearly 52 miles) per day, Strel was not put off by the dangers of piranha, caimans, or anacondas on his epic swim.

Explorers in the rainforest need to be not easily put off by poisonous animals and plants.

WHO'S GOING WITH YOU?

The rainforests are a fascinating but dangerous place. You'll need people who understand this delicate environment and who can keep you safe while you explore it. Here are some of the best people in history to help you.

Expedition member: Alexander von Humboldt (1769–1859)

Alexander von Humboldt was a pioneer in the study of nature and spent several years exploring the Amazon rainforest. He was one of the first people to realize that cutting down forests could affect climate. He is also an expert on weather and rocks.

Potential job: Expedition naturalist

Expedition member: Local guide

When exploring the rainforest, local knowledge is essential. You want to know which plants might be safe to eat, which animals to look out for, and you also need someone to help you communicate with the people you find. More than 3,000 languages are spoken in rainforests around the world, some of them by just a few isolated groups.

Potential job: Guide

Expedition member:
Mary Kingsley
(1862–1900)

If you're looking for an intrepid explorer, Mary Kingsley won't give up. In the 1890s, women were not expected to explore the African rainforests on their own, but Kingsley refused to follow the rules, even when she fell into a pit dug as a trap by **cannibals**. Her thick Victorian dress saved her from the spikes at the bottom.

Potential job:
Leading explorer

Expedition member: Specialist in tropical medicine

You need a good doctor as you may have to face many tropical diseases or poisonous animals. Deep in the rainforest, your expedition will probably be a long way from the nearest hospital.

Potential job: Expedition doctor

SEEING THE SIGHTS

The noise and colour of the rainforest can be quite bewildering. If you want to understand what's going on in the forest, you need to divide the forest into different layers from top to bottom. There are plenty of living things to explore in each layer.

Different layers of the rainforest

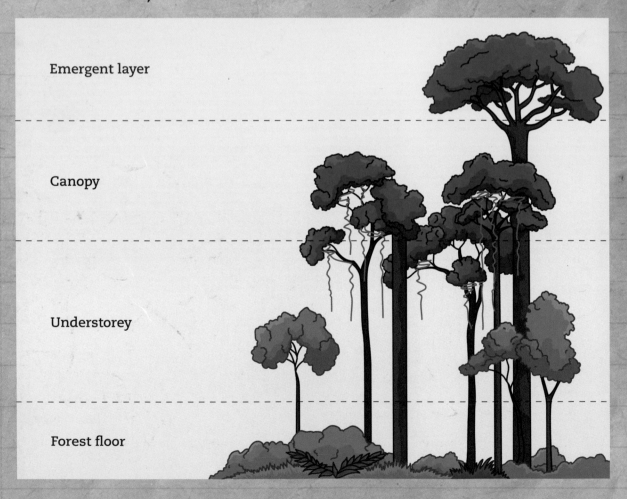

Emergent layer

Canopy

Understorey

Forest floor

Around three-quarters of rainforest animals live in the canopy.

The canopy

The green roof of the forest is called the canopy. Most rainforest trees grow to a similar height and this canopy is home to birds and climbing animals such as monkeys and sloths. A few trees poke above the level of the canopy in the **emergent layer** of the forest. These are the tallest rainforest trees, towering 60 metres (200 feet) above the forest floor.

 Conservation

You may find large areas of rainforest with no trees. Rainforest trees are in great demand, particularly for their hard woods that are used to make furniture. Trees are also cut down to make room for grazing animals. These trees took many decades to grow. Once a grove of trees is lost, it will never grow back. And once the trees are gone, the soil hardens and the amount of rain can decrease.

The understorey

All around you beneath the canopy you will find the **understorey**. This damp, shady area is home to smaller trees and shrubs. The trees' growth is held back because the canopy blocks much of the essential sunlight from reaching them.

Amazing facts

Vampire bats will normally only hunt at night in South America's rainforests. They will creep up on their sleeping prey, make a hole with their sharp teeth, and eat the blood that oozes out.

Can you spot any **epiphytes**? Don't worry, this is just a scientific word for any plants that are growing on or attached to other plants. Instead of getting nutrients from the soil, epiphytes get them directly from the air. The understorey is packed with ferns and beautiful orchids that cling to other trees and plants.

Understorey animals

You will find plenty of birds, insects, and tree frogs living in the trees and shrubs of the understorey. Keep a close eye on the low branches. They might be a handy resting place for a jaguar or a boa constrictor snake waiting for its next meal to walk by.

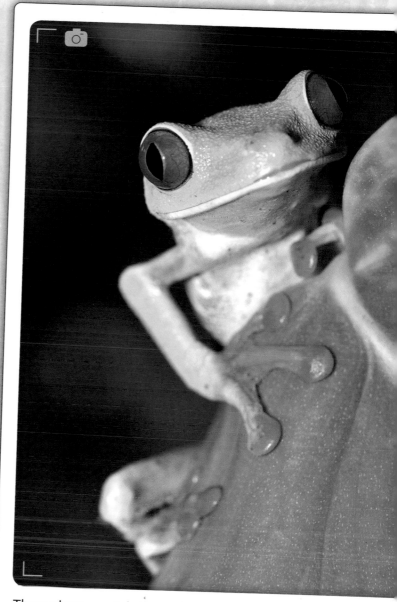

The understorey is home to beautiful tree frogs, but some of them can be deadly poisonous for the careless explorer.

Conservation

Rainforests are home to many species of **amphibians**, such as frogs and toads. Amphibians live both on land and in water. Logging and loss of rainforests are one reason why more than 40 per cent of amphibian species are under threat of extinction.

INTERVIEW WITH A RAINFOREST EXPLORER

← Dr Margaret (Meg) Lowman has been called the "Einstein of the treetops" for her pioneering work exploring the canopy of rainforests around the world. You can find out more about her work at www.canopymeg.com.

Q: When did you first become interested in rainforests?

A: When I was a child, I climbed trees in my backyard, looking at bird nests, watching beetles eat leaves, and finding new discoveries in nature. As a field biologist, I discovered early in my career that no one knew very much about treetops. Most people walk through the woods, including scientists, and only look at the ground or the very lowest part of a tree trunk.

Q: What's so special about the canopy in a rainforest?

A: The canopy is sometimes called the "eighth continent" of the world, meaning that it is a new region for exploration. Scientists estimate that almost half of the world's biodiversity lives in the treetops, and we probably have identified and named less than 10 per cent.

Q: How do you study the canopy?

A: As a student, I sewed a harness and carved a slingshot to propel myself into the canopy using ropes and climbing hardware. I have since tried hot-air balloons, canopy walkways, construction cranes, treehouses, cherry-pickers, and other creative tools to enter into this magical world of the treetops. Today, I have a small company and foundation (www.treefoundation.org) that builds canopy walkways. Walkways are important for eco-tourism and allowing people to learn and appreciate their local forests instead of cutting them down.

Q: What's left to explore in the rainforest?

A: A friend of mine has devoted his entire life to answering a question, "What is the commonest tree in the tropical rainforest?" No one even knows the answer to that basic question. A recent challenge in my work is to measure the insect poo falling from the canopy to the forest floor. This is an important element of nutrient cycling, but to date no scientist has successfully collected and extracted the relatively tiny pieces of insect waste material that looks almost identical to the many other particles falling down to the forest floor.

RAINFOREST LIVING

At least half of all animal and plant species are found in the rainforest. You can learn a lot about surviving in the rainforest by watching these animals. Almost all animals live in fear of predators. Even a fearsome crocodile can be strangled by a giant anaconda. Animals have adapted to survive in the rainforest, such as tree frogs that are brightly coloured to warn predators that they are poisonous to eat.

Jaguars use their spotted fur as **camouflage** to merge into the forest.

Don't forget

The rainforest is a great source of natural foods, but you need to know what you can safely eat:

- Don't eat anything raw unless you are certain what it is.
- Edible fruits include those from the yarina and aguaje palm tree, as well as more familiar things such as passion fruit.
- When aguaje fruits fall to the ground, you can find beetle **grubs** inside. Chop off the black heads of the white grubs and eat the bodies raw or cooked on a fire. Delicious!

Complex ecosystems

Living things in the rainforest, including explorers, rely on other living things to survive. The Brazil nut tree is one of the largest trees in the Amazon, but it is pollinated by the orchid bee. These bees depend on the sweet perfume of orchids to attract a mate. Brazil nut trees also need tiny squirrel-like agoutis, which are the only animals with teeth sharp enough to break open the Brazil nut cases and so plant new trees.

Pools of water collecting in these plants can be home to tiny living things. Hummingbirds and butterflies rely on nectar from their flowers.

 ## Conservation

Many rainforest species rely on each other in complex relationships. When one species of plant or animal disappears because of forest being cleared or climate change, this may affect many other species that rely on it for food or protection from predators.

Weird and wonderful

With so much amazing life in the rainforest, you would expect to find some really weird animals – you won't be disappointed. Here are a few that you might see on your travels.

Sloths are not always easy to spot as they hang upside-down in the canopy. Their reputation for being the most laid-back animals in the forest is well deserved. They can actually swim faster than they can walk. Sloths move so slowly that tiny plants called algae have time to grow on their fur.

Amazing facts

If you see a sloth on the ground, it's probably come down to go to the toilet, which it does every six days or so. That's one thing you shouldn't do while hanging upside down!

An aye-aye is a type of lemur. Lemurs are only found in the wild on Madagascar.

On islands such as Madagascar, in the Indian Ocean, animals are more isolated than in **continental** rainforest. This leads to unusual creatures such as the aye-aye, which is only found on the island. An aye-aye uses its long middle fingers to tap tree trunks and search for bugs to eat. When it finds them, it uses its fingers to dig them out of the bark.

Massive minibeasts

If you don't like bugs, rainforest exploring is not for you. One of the scariest is the Goliath bird-eating spider, which can be 30 centimetres (12 inches) across, with fangs 2.5 centimetres (1 inch) long. Although they can eat a small bird or rodent, they usually eat other minibeasts.

Who's who

British naturalist Alfred Russel Wallace (1823–1913) developed the theory of evolution around the same time as the more famous Charles Darwin. Wallace developed his ideas during many years travelling in the Amazon rainforest and Southeast Asia. His Amazon journey ended in tragedy in 1852, when a fire on the ship taking Wallace home destroyed thousands of specimens gathered in the rainforest.

PEOPLE AND THE RAINFOREST

There are more than 20 million people living in the Amazon, mainly in cities, and millions more living in rainforests around the world. Many of these people live in towns and cities but around 180,000 people in the Amazon live a traditional life, which depends on the forest.

There are just a few thousand Kayapo people living deep in the Brazilian rainforest.

According to the organization Survival International, there are probably around 100 tribes across the world that have chosen not to have any contact with outsiders. Most of these people are believed to live in the forests of South America or Southeast Asia. Could you be the explorer to discover these people of the rainforest? If so, you should be aware of the dangers you bring. In the past, illnesses and germs that explorers from other continents brought with them killed millions of **indigenous** people.

Indigenous people will be able to tell you most about what it's like to live in the forest, but they also have good reasons to be wary of outsiders.

Amazing facts

Waimiri Atroari people of Brazil use 32 different types of plant just to make their hunting equipment.

Conservation

The Kayapo people live deep in the Amazon rainforest. They use more than 600 different plants for food and medicines. They also plant fruit and Brazil nut trees, which they can harvest every year. It is said that Kayapo children know so much about the forest that they can name 60 different types of bee. Working with the forest helps to preserve and renew it, as well as to feed the Kayapo people.

Industry and exploitation

When you're exploring the rainforest you will see many signs of the ways in which people and industry are damaging the forests.

Forest trees are not just cut down for timber. Large areas of rainforest have been cleared to make room for animals to graze. These animals satisfy the world's growing demand for meat.

In some rainforest areas, crops such as soya and oil palms are taking over where rainforest used to grow.

 Who's who

Chico Mendes (1944–1988) was a rubber tapper in the Brazilian rainforest. He extracted natural rubber from trees. In the 1980s, Mendes opposed the clearing of rainforest trees by cattle ranchers, and the effect it had on traditional ways of life. His campaign earned Mendes worldwide fame but that could not protect him from the powerful people he opposed. Mendes was shot dead in 1988.

Today's rainforest explorers will also come across much more industry than earlier travellers would have seen. Mines for metal and other minerals have been dug in the forest and the search is also on for oil beneath the forests.

Gone forever

Farms and mines provide work for people who are often extremely poor. However, the forest and its delicate ecosystems have grown up over hundreds or thousands of years. The effects of this damage to the rainforests are felt far away from where the forest is actually being cleared.

Conservation

The world's rainforests are being destroyed at a rate of about 100,000 square kilometres (40,000 square miles) every year. That's an area bigger than Scotland. The good news is that **deforestation** in the Amazon rainforest fell in 2011 to its lowest level for many years.

This rainforest in Peru is being cleared so the land can be used for farming.

INTERVIEW WITH A CONSERVATION EXPERT

← David Gill is Programme Officer in the Conservation Science team with Fauna & Flora International, which aims to conserve rainforests by working with the people who live there.

Q: Tell us about your work in the rainforest.

A: I've been fortunate enough to work in two very different rainforests. In Paraguay, I was based in the poorly known Atlantic Forest – a **fragmented** ecosystem surrounded by a sea of soya fields. Searching for reptiles at day and recording the calls of several frog species at night, I helped identify some of the forest's remaining biodiversity. In Equatorial Guinea, in central Africa, the forest is dense, covers great mountains, and is home to gorillas and forest elephants. My work here was very different, living with local hunters to understand why and how they hunted, and what impacts changing hunting methods were having on forest wildlife.

Q: When did you first become interested in the rainforests?

A: Ever since I watched my first David Attenborough documentary as a child; but my time in Paraguay, encountering a huge diversity of species, left a huge impression on me.

Q: Why is rainforest biodiversity important?

A: For every species we lose, we lose a part of the rainforest "machine" that we absolutely need to be in working order to keep the rest of the world's climate in check. All species in a rainforest are connected in some way and the more biodiversity we lose the more likely we are to lose a key part of these great ecosystems.

Q: What one change would you make to protect rainforests?

A: Rainforests are being converted at an alarming rate to crops such as soya and palm used in biofuels and many of our day-to-day foods. We can't expect developing countries to control rainforest destruction unless we can control our own consumption; one very simple change would be to reduce the amount of food we waste in the developed world.

Q: Do you have any advice for rainforest explorers?

A: Take time to look at the little things. Within a patch of forest the size of your garden, you can find thousands of insects and hundreds of plants. We have so much to learn about these species.

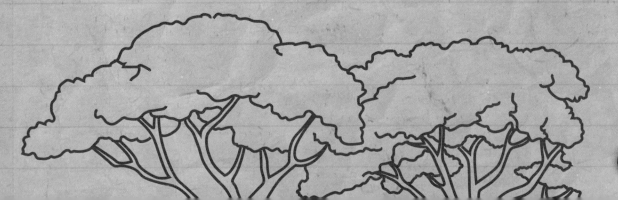

ARE THE RAINFORESTS CHANGING?

Enjoy your visit to the rainforests, because the next time you go there things could be very different. Rainforests are always changing because a rainforest is made up of living things, which are growing all the time. The rainforest would not exist at all without the hot sun and heavy rain all year round.

Although the loss of rainforest areas has slowed, it is still a major problem, particularly in Southeast Asia where rainforests could disappear in the next few decades. Climate change also poses major threats to the rainforest.

Conservation

Governments and campaigners do not want to save rainforests so a few explorers can go and see the trees and animals. However, rainforests are the richest ecosystems on the planet. We know that Earth will be much poorer without them. Rainforests are called the "lungs of the world" because they take carbon dioxide from the atmosphere and release oxygen, to help reduce climate change.

Amazing facts

The scarlet macaw has huge wings and can fly at 56 kilometres (35 miles) an hour!

The explorer's mission

The job for today's explorers is to get people thinking about the incredible wealth and value of the rainforest. Discovering new places and new species can convince people that we cannot live without rainforests.

You can marvel at beautiful creatures like this scarlet macaw, but don't disturb their habitat or try to take them home with you.

Don't forget

Here are some rules to follow so you can explore rainforests without harming them:

- Do not harm animals or plants, or take souvenirs home with you.
- Take your rubbish home with you. Any litter could poison animals.
- Respect the cultures and history of people who live in the rainforest, and follow their advice about living with the forest.

WORLD MAP

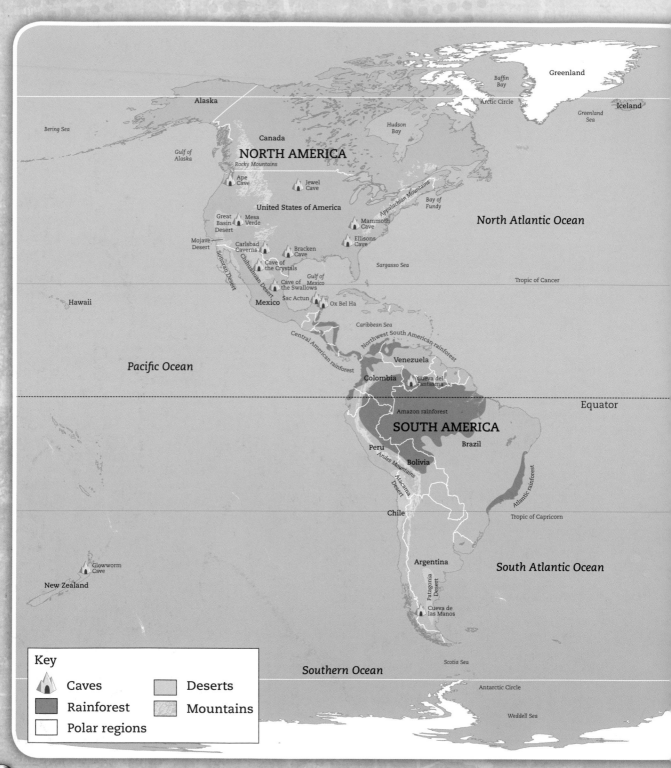

Greenland

Baffin
Bay

Arctic Circle

Iceland

Greenland
Sea

Alaska

Bering Sea

Gulf of
Alaska

Hudson
Bay

Canada

NORTH AMERICA

Rocky Mountains

Ape
Cave

Jewel
Cave

Appalachian Mountains

Bay of
Fundy

North Atlantic Ocean

United States of America

Great
Basin
Desert

Mesa
Verde

Mammoth
Cave

Mojave
Desert

Carlsbad
Caverns

Bracken
Cave

Ellisons
Cave

Sargasso Sea

Cave of
the Crystals

Sonoran Desert

Chihuahuan Desert

Cave of
the Swallows

Gulf of
Mexico

Tropic of Cancer

Hawaii

Mexico

Sac Actun

Ox Bel Ha

Caribbean Sea

Central American rainforest

Northwest South American rainforest

Pacific Ocean

Venezuela

Colombia

Cueva del
Fantasma

Amazon rainforest

Equator

SOUTH AMERICA

Peru

Brazil

Andes Mountains

Bolivia

Atacama
Desert

Atlantic rainforest

Chile

Tropic of Capricorn

Glowworm
Cave

Argentina

South Atlantic Ocean

New Zealand

Patagonia
Desert

Cueva de
las Manos

Scotia Sea

Southern Ocean

Antarctic Circle

Weddell Sea

Key

- ▲ Caves
- ▨ Deserts
- ▨ Rainforest
- ▨ Mountains
- ▢ Polar regions

EXPLORER **TRAVEL** GUIDES

This map shows you where to find some of the world's rainforests. There are many other exciting places to discover. Why not explore the oceans, caves, deserts, and mountains shown on the map?

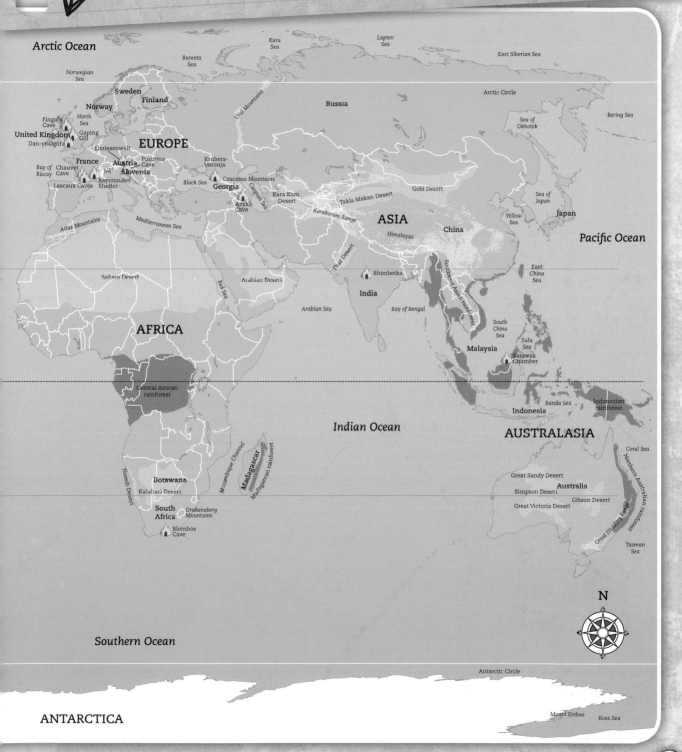

Arctic Ocean

Kara Sea

Laptev Sea

East Siberian Sea

Barents Sea

Norwegian Sea

Arctic Circle

Sweden

Finland

Russia

Bering Sea

Norway

North Sea

Sea of Okhotsk

Fingal's Cave

United Kingdom

Gaping Gill

Dan-yr-Ogof

Eisriesenwelt

EUROPE

Ural Mountains

Krubera-Voronja

Postojna Cave

Bay of Biscay

France

Chauvet Cave

Austria

Alps

Slovenia

Black Sea

Caucasus Mountains

Georgia

Sea of Japan

Japan

Lascaux Caves

Raymonden Shelter

Azykh Cave

Caspian Sea

Kara Kum Desert

Karakoram Range

Takla Makan Desert

Gobi Desert

Yellow Sea

East China Sea

Pacific Ocean

Atlas Mountains

Mediterranean Sea

ASIA

China

Red Sea

Sahara Desert

Arabian Desert

Thar Desert

Himalayas

Bhimbetka

Southeast Asian rainforest

AFRICA

Arabian Sea

India

Bay of Bengal

South China Sea

Sulu Sea

Sarawak Chamber

Malaysia

Central African rainforest

Indian Ocean

Banda Sea

Indonesia

Indonesian rainforest

AUSTRALASIA

Coral Sea

Mozambique Channel

Madagascar

Madagascan rainforest

Namib Desert

Botswana

Kalahari Desert

Great Sandy Desert

Simpson Desert

Australia

Gibson Desert

Northern Australian rainforest

South Africa

Drakensberg Mountains

Great Victoria Desert

Great Dividing Range

Tasman Sea

Blombos Cave

N

Southern Ocean

Antarctic Circle

ANTARCTICA

Mount Erebus

Ross Sea

TIMELINE

1541	Spaniard Francisco de Orellana leads the first European expedition through the Amazon rainforest
1595	Sir Walter Raleigh leads an expedition up the Orinoco River into the rainforest in search of "El Dorado"
1799	Alexander von Humboldt begins a five-year journey to the forests of Central and South America
1820	The drug quinine, used to treat malaria, is first extracted from the cinchona tree that grows in rainforests
1874	Henry Morton Stanley begins his journey down the River Congo through Africa's rainforest
1893	Mary Kingsley travels to West Africa and along the Gabon River
1941	Richard Schultes makes his first journey to the Amazon rainforest to show how the region's people use plants as medicines
1962	Belem-Brasilia Highway becomes the first major road to cross the Amazon rainforest
1988	Chico Mendes is shot dead, ending his campaign to protect the Amazon rainforest from exploitation
1992	Rio de Janeiro, Brazil hosts the Earth Summit, at which the world's governments agree a Convention on Biological Diversity
2010	Explorer Ed Stafford completes a 6,437-kilometre (4,500-mile) walk along the River Amazon
2011	Destruction of Brazilian rainforest is measured at its lowest level in 23 years

FACT FILE

THE WORLD'S TROPICAL RAINFORESTS

	Area	Countries	Forest fact
Amazon rainforest	6.7 million square kilometres (2.6 million square miles)	Brazil, Peru, Bolivia, Colombia, Ecuador, Guyana, Suriname, Venezuela, French Guiana	In some places, annual rainfall is more than 800 metres (26 feet)
Central African rainforest	1.8 million square kilometres (700,000 square miles)	Central Africa from Cameroon and Gabon to Burundi	Home to the largest land mammal – the African elephant
Southeast Asian rainforest	1.7 million square kilometres (650,000 square miles)	Burma, Laos, Cambodia, Malaysia, Thailand, Vietnam	Tallest trees reach heights of 50 metres (160 feet)
Indonesian rainforest	1.45 million square kilometres (560,000 square miles)	Indonesia	Home to the Rafflesia, which produces the largest flower of any plant
Madagascan rainforest	38,000 square kilometres (15,000 square miles)	Madagascar	80 per cent of plant species in Madagascar are found nowhere else
Northern Australian rainforest	10,500 square kilometres (4,000 square miles)	Australia	Home to two species of tree kangaroos

- The trees of a tropical rainforest are so densely packed together in the canopy that rain can take 10 minutes to reach the ground.

- More than 4,000 different species of butterfly have been found in the rainforests of South America, and a single hectare of rainforest can contain 20,000 beetle species.

- If you live in the western United States or Canada, or parts of Australia and New Zealand, you might live near a temperate rainforest. These are very different from tropical rainforests, but they have huge trees and many native animal species.

GLOSSARY

amphibian animal that spends part of its life in water and part on land. Frogs and toads are amphibians.

atmosphere layer of gases surrounding Earth, made of a mixture of gases that humans and living things need to breathe

bacteria microscopic organisms that help to break down dead organic matter

biodiversity variety of living things found on Earth or in an ecosystem such as the rainforest

botanist scientist who studies plants

camouflage colour or pattern on an animal's skin or fur that allows it to blend into the background

cannibal person that eats humans

canopy layer in a rainforest formed by the branches and leaves of trees

capsize when a boat tips over on to its side

carbon dioxide gas that is released when organic materials such as wood or coal are burned. Too much carbon dioxide in the atmosphere causes the climate to get warmer.

civilization society where people live in settled communities and have a certain culture or way of life

climate change gradual increase in temperature on Earth, mainly caused by human actions such as burning fossil fuels

cloud forest mountain rainforest that is usually covered with low cloud or fog

conquistador name given to Spanish adventurers who explored and invaded Central and South America

continental on a continent, rather than an isolated island

deforestation process by which forests are destroyed

ecosystem environment such as the rainforest and the animals and plants that live in it

emergent layer top layer of rainforest made up of trees that break out over the canopy

epiphyte plant that grows on another object or plant

fragmented broken up

fungus (plural: **fungi**) group of organisms that feed on animal and plant material, including mushrooms and toadstools

grub larva or young of an insect

humid hot and damp

indigenous people who come from a particular place, rather than people who moved there from somewhere else

malaria tropical disease carried by mosquitoes that affects millions of people around the world

mammal warm-blooded animal that usually has fur or hair and drinks milk from its mother when it is young. Humans, whales, and dolphins are mammals.

orchid type of plant that produces beautiful and colourful flowers

oxygen gas in the atmosphere that humans and animals need to breathe

parasite organism that lives on and feeds off another living thing

predator animal that hunts or eats other animals

prey animal that is hunted by another animal for food

species group of organisms that are similar and are able to produce offspring together

specimen plant or animal that is used as an example of its species

suffocate prevent a living thing from breathing, which can lead to death

temperate rainforest forest in cooler regions that receives very heavy rain

tropical referring to the tropics, which is the area of Earth either side of the equator

understorey level of rainforest beneath the main canopy and above the ground

FIND OUT MORE

Books

Bloomin' Rainforests (Horrible Geography), Anita Ganeri (Scholastic, 2008)

Great Explorers, Jim Pipe (OUP, 2008)

Rainforest Animals (Saving Wildlife), Sonya Newland (Franklin Watts, 2010)

Rainforests (Planet Earth), Steve Parker (QED, 2009)

Websites

www.arf.net.au

The Australian Rainforest Foundation works to protect Australia's rainforest.

www.arkive.org

This fantastic site is full of information and videos about animals from rainforests and many other habitats.

www.edstafford.org

Find out about Ed Stafford's amazing journey through the Amazon rainforest.

www.fauna-flora.org

Fauna & Flora International is a conservation group that works in many locations to preserve biodiversity.

www.passporttoknowledge.com/rainforest/main.html

Explore the rainforest, guided by some of the world's leading scientists.

www.rgs.org

The Royal Geographical Society focuses on geography, education, fieldwork, and expeditions.

Places to visit

You may not live near a rainforest, but you can always explore the animals and plants in your nearest forest. You may also be able to visit one of the following places to see rainforest plants and animals.

Kew Gardens

London

www.kew.org

Kew is home to a huge range of plants, including rainforest plants in the Palm House and indoor conservatories.

The Eden Project

Bodelva, St Austell

Cornwall PL24 2SG

www.edenproject.com

The Eden Project is the world's largest indoor greenhouse, where you can be amazed by the range of rainforest trees and plants.

The Living Rainforest

Hampstead Norreys

Berkshire RG10 0TN

www.livingrainforest.org

The Living Rainforest is a dramatic collection of rare rainforest plants and creatures.

Further research

- Find out about scientists currently working in the rainforest. News websites will tell you about the latest discoveries.
- Research the lives of people who live in the rainforest. How do they work to preserve the environment where they live?
- Rainforests have a vital role in preventing climate change. Discover more about the fight against global warming.

INDEX

EXPLORER TRAVEL GUIDES

RAINFORESTS

Nick Hunter

Raintree

Raintree is an imprint of Capstone Global Library Limited, a company incorporated in England and Wales having its registered office at 7 Pilgrim Street, London, EC4V 6LB – Registered company number: 6695582

www.raintreepublishers.co.uk
myorders@raintreepublishers.co.uk

Text © Capstone Global Library Limited 2014
First published in hardback in 2014
Paperback edition first published in 2015
The moral rights of the proprietor have been asserted.

Edited by Adam Miller, Laura Knowles, and Claire Throp
Designed by Steve Mead
Original illustrations © Capstone Global Library Ltd 2014
Illustrated by H L Studios
Picture research by Tracy Cummins
Production by Victoria Fitzgerald
Originated by Capstone Global Library Ltd
Printed in China by China Translation and Printing Services

ISBN 978 1 406 26014 4 (hardback)
17 16 15 14 13
10 9 8 7 6 5 4 3 2 1

ISBN 978 1 406 26021 2 (paperback)
18 17 16 15 14
10 9 8 7 6 5 4 3 2 1

British Library Cataloguing in Publication Data
Hunter, Nick
Rainforests. – (Explorer travel guides)
910.9'152-dc23
A full catalogue record for this book is available from the British Library.

Acknowledgements

We would like to thank the following for permission to reproduce photographs: Alamy p. 13 (© David Tomlinson); Corbis pp. 15 (© Frans Lantin), 16 (© Ian Nichols/National Geographic Society); Fauna & Flora International p. 36 (David Gill); Getty Images pp. 4 (Ed George), 5 bottom, 34 (Jason Isley – Scubazoo), 11 (Pete Mcbride/National Geographic), 14 (Hulton Archive), 19 (Time & Life Pictures), 21 (simonlong), 24 (Gail Shumway), 30 (Roy Toft), 31 (David Haring/DUPC), 32 (Cristina Mittermeier/National Geographic); Nasa p. 8 (Jesse Allen/ courtesy of the University of Maryland's Global Land Cover Facility); Newscom p. 26 (ZUMA Press); Shutterstock pp. 5 middle, 23, 39 (© worldswildlifewonders), 5 top, 10 (© Vadim Petrakov), 6 (© Mike Price), 7 (© David Good), 9 (© GlobetrotterJ), 28 (© Rechitan Sorin), 29, 35 (© Dr. Morley Read); Superstock pp. 17 (© age fotostock), 22 (© Barry Mansell), 25 (© Minden Pictures).

Design elements: Shutterstock (© szefei), (© Nik Merkulov), (© vovan), (© SmileStudio), (© Petrov Stanislav Eduardovich), (© Nataliia Natykach), (© Phecsone).

Cover photograph of the tropical rainforest canopy at dawn, in the Maliau Basin, Sabah, Borneo, East Malaysia reproduced with permission of Getty Images (Jason Isley – Scubazoo).

We would like to thank Daniel Block for his invaluable help in the preparation of this book.

Every effort has been made to contact copyright holders of material reproduced in this book. Any omissions will be rectified in subsequent printings if notice is given to the publisher.

Disclaimer

All the internet addresses (URLs) given in this book were valid at the time of going to press. However, due to the dynamic nature of the internet, some addresses may have changed, or sites may have changed or ceased to exist since publication. While the author and publisher regret any inconvenience this may cause readers, no responsibility for any such changes can be accepted by either the author or the publisher.